TEACHING
the
LORD'S PRAYER

Delia Halverson

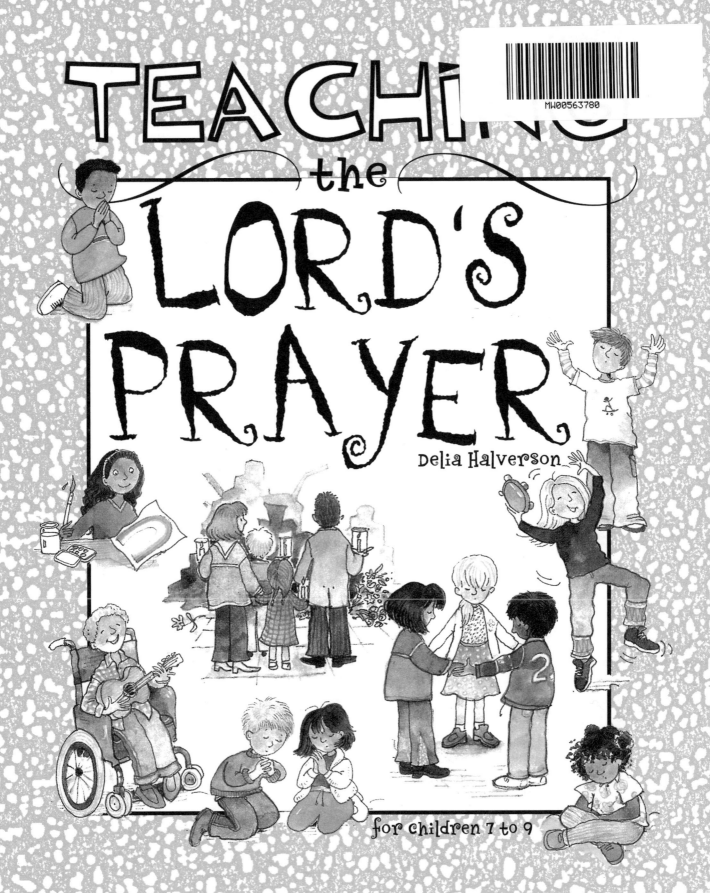

for children 7 to 9

Teaching the Lord's Prayer

Scripture quotations are from the New Revised Standard Version of the Bible. Copyright © 1989 by the Division of Christian Education of the National Council of Churches of Christ in the U.S.A. Used by permission.

Scripture quotations identified as Contemporary English Version are from the *Contemporary English Version,* Copyright © American Bible Society 1991, 1992.

Cover Art: Paula Martyr/Linden Artists LTD. From *Exploring Faith: Middle Elementary, Student, Winter 2002-03.* © 2002 Cokesbury.

"The Lord's Prayer" used in this publication can be found in *The United Methodist Hymnal,* #895.

ISBN 0-687-06294-2

04 05 06 07 08 09 10 11 12 13 – 10 9 8 7 6 5 4 3 2 1

Manufactured in the United States of America

Table of Contents

Introduction

Why Do We Teach the Lord's Prayer?

From early in life, we hope that our children will learn the words and pray the Lord's Prayer with us. It is important for them to feel a part of the worshiping community and pray the prayer with the church family, whether they understand the words or not at that point. By the time they are of middle and older elementary age, however, they can begin to comprehend the meaning behind the words. This is when we need an in-depth study to bring new meaning to the words. We do not, however, want to teach them to parrot some other person's interpretation of the prayer. We want them to think through the meaning themselves. That is how they really internalize the prayer.

You will find that some children have heard these words all their lives, and hopefully parents have helped them comprehend some of the meaning. For those children, this study will help them grow deeper in their prayer life. For those who have not been introduced to the meaning behind the words, this may open new doors to their understanding. Rejoice in the opportunity before you, to work with this beautiful prayer that Jesus gave us and share it with the children!

The prayer is important, not just because Jesus gave it to us, but because it is a model that will help us all pray our own prayers. During the sessions children will also learn to use their own words to pray, using parts of this prayer as a model.

TEACHING THESE LESSONS:

The six sessions in this book all have the same format. Your class time and space, as well as your students', will make a difference in just what you choose to do in each section. However, I would strongly urge that you follow the format by using something from each section.

It is important that you read the background information that is provided before each session plan. This will give you thoughts and insights that will be helpful as you discuss parts of the prayer with your students.

Where there is discussion, try using a bean bag or a similar object to control the discussion. The bean bag is tossed to the person who has permission to talk, and only the person with the bean bag talks at that time. Then it is passed on to the next person who talks in the discussion. This not only eliminates extra voices in the discussion, but it centers the listeners to the person speaking.

GATHERING:

These activities will include opportunities for the students to get acquainted during the first two sessions and will have some activities in each session that may be used as the students arrive. It will also include any preparation activities for the rest of the session. When the students help to prepare the room or prepare themselves to assist with the teaching, they become an integral part of the learning.

EXPERIENCE PRAYER:

Any study of the Lord's Prayer should naturally include prayer. During the first session the subject of prayer will be introduced, and each session will include opportunity for group prayer during this time. This section of each session will also include one way of learning the Lord's Prayer itself. By experimenting with various methods, we hope to hit some method that is beneficial to each student.

CENTER ON THE PHRASE:

This section of the study will center on a specific section of the prayer each session. There will be learning activities that help to bring a deeper meaning to that section of the prayer. Choose at least one of these activities for your group, depending on your time.

CENTER ON LIFE:

This section brings the Lord's Prayer into the life of the student. There will be activities that relate the phrase you are studying that week to some part of the student's everyday life. Choose at least one of these activities for your group, depending on your time.

PRAYER AND PRAISE:

This is the climax of the session and should always be included. It will center around a Celebration Table that students have helped arrange during the Gathering Time. Each prayer and praise time will have participation by some individual(s) in the class. Be sure that you give ample time for this section, giving warning ahead so that any individual activities can be completed (or set aside to take home for completion) in time to come to the Celebration Table.

HOW WE LEARN:

Perhaps you never learned the Lord's Prayer any other way than by rote. That is probably the only way that most of our children have been introduced to it. However, God made each of us different, and God gave each of us unique ways to learn. God didn't cut us all out with a cookie cutter! Each person learns in his or her own way. It is particularly important to remember the various learning styles as we teach elementary children and youth. Although educators have only recently distinguished them, our various ways of learning have been a part of humanity from the beginning. Jesus used all of these methods of teaching in his ministry. Listed below are the various methods and examples from Jesus' life.

Verbal/Linguistic - has to do with language and words, both written and spoken. Jesus approached his listeners in this manner with his stories.

Logical/Mathematical - has to do with inductive thinking and reasoning, statistics, and abstract patterns. Jesus used questions and answers to reach his listeners who learned this way.

Visual/Spatial - has to do with visualizing objects and creating internal mental pictures. Jesus used common objects to explain his meanings to persons who learn in this manner.

Body/Kinesthetic - related to the physical, such as movement and physical activity. Jesus involved disciples in learning by fishing and washing their feet.

Musical/Rhythmic - involves recognition of patterns, both tonal and rhythmic. Singing hymns was a part of the common experience of Jesus and his disciples.

Interpersonal - follows relationships between persons, including true communication. Jesus worked with persons on a personal level and also developed small group settings, his most successful being the twelve disciples.

Intrapersonal - primarily through self-reflection and awareness of that within us that guides us. Many times the Bible mentions Jesus drawing away for solitude or to be by himself (or taking his disciples away) for reflection.

Nature - use of nature in learning. Jesus used nature in many of his illustrations. He taught in the out-of-doors most of the time.

PRACTICE PRAYER YOURSELF:

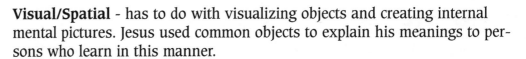

As we teach, we teachers learn even more than our students. Your prayer life will be enriched as you prepare and teach these lessons. However, don't rely on the prep time and teaching times as your only spiritual enrichment. In order to convey the real meaning of this prayer, you need to steep yourself in prayer too. You need to move into an intimate relationship with God.

Practicing prayer is important for all teachers, but it is especially important for you as you teach this classic prayer that Jesus taught. Just as each person has a different mode of learning, each person has his or her own way to grow spiritually. We are beginning to realize that this may hinge on our personalities. You might try some of these possibilities as you spend time in personal prayer.

Meditate on a picture or object – empty your mind of all else and center on the picture and object, keeping open to what God may be saying to you at the time.

Pray with your senses – use objects that you can smell, taste, touch, hear, and see as you pray.

Musical prayers – use a recording of a song or hymn to pray. Pay attention to the words as well as the music.

Journal with Scripture – select a Scripture or inspirational reading and write down any thoughts that come to your mind as you read it several times.

Journal on life – review what has happened to you that particular day including conversations you had with others, and write down where you have seen God evident in your life.

Breath prayer – develop a brief sentence prayer that can be said in one breath and use it frequently during the day.

Passing prayers – make yourself aware of people and things around you and consciously say a prayer as you encounter them.

Although we do not want to make praying such a routine experience that it becomes mundane, we sometimes need some sort of prayer pattern to get started. Here is a suggestion you may want to try.

Prepare yourself. Find a location that is comfortable, where you will not be disturbed. Luke tells us that Jesus "would go away to lonely places, where he prayed."

Repeat a simple verse or prayer. Learn a short Bible verse or prayer or song. Breathe slowly for several seconds, being conscious of your breathing, and then repeat the verse or prayer, or sing the song quietly.

Accept God into your heart. To do this, center into the very heart of you. Consider the part of you that feels love, that feels sadness, the part that is happy when you do for others. Then ask God to come into that part of you.

Yield all that bothers you to God. Whatever is troubling you, turn it over to God. Know that God understands your problems.

Enjoy God's presence. Just spend some time "looking and loving" God. Feel God's strength and peace.

Review how you felt. Consider a prayer journal, writing down some of the feelings and thoughts that came to you as you prayed.

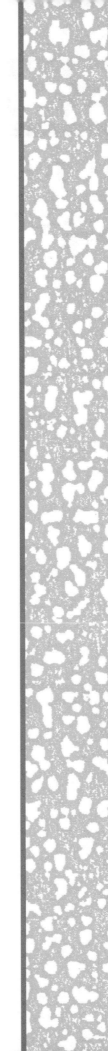

SESSION 1

What does it mean to worship God?

NOTE:

Before you begin, read the introduction, particularly the information on page 6 titled "Teaching These Lessons."

Our Father who art in heaven, hallowed be thy name.

BACKGROUND:

The first three phrases (Our Father, who art in heaven, hallowed by thy name.) of the prayer parallel the opening words of the ancient Jewish Kaddish, a prayer that is recited daily for loved ones who have died. It is recited during the first year after a person's death. Jesus used the phrases to help the disciples form their own prayers.

The first two phrases that we will work with in this session help us think of what it means to worship God. Speaking of God as holy (or hallowed) and at the same time a personal God may seem strange. But that combination is the heart of this prayer—God is holy but yearns to be in relationship with us. This is why prayer is so important, because it deepens our relationship with God.

The word for father that Jesus used was "Abba," which would more literally be translated as "Daddy." It is a very personal term. You may have some students who do not have a good relationship with their father, and the word may draw up negative images. Be aware of this and help all of your students think of God as the most loving parent they can imagine, either a mother or a father, or some other parent they may know. Not a parent that just gives gifts, but one that loves them in a personal way.

The word "hallowed" speaks of worshiping God. The word "worship" is often specified to the acts of worship on Sunday morning. We limit it to the specific order of worship, which is "liturgy." Liturgy can be defined as "the work of the people," and in corporate worship we need to recognize that we, the people, are in the act of worshiping God, not in a spectator posture. But worship goes farther than simply sitting in a service on Sunday morning. Worship is adoration or devotion to God. It is an expression of awe, and it can happen any time and at any place. It is recognizing that God is so awesome that we cannot even imagine the depth of God's being. But in the same instance, as Jesus taught us, we can see God as very personal, like a very close parent who is loving and wants the best for a child and wants to be loved in return.

Often we believe we should know instinctively how to pray, and we feel inadequate when we don't. From the question that the disciples asked Jesus, we see that even the disciples needed help praying, although they were constant companions of Jesus and heard him pray every day.

In answer, Jesus gave the disciples a personal way to pray to God. Praying to God in a personal manner was not common at that time. There were set rituals for prayer, and God was regarded as very distant—in the heavens. Sacrifices were considered necessary to appease God or to bring God closer in order to hear us. The Gospels often speak of Jesus praying, but there is no mention of Jesus giving sacrifices. In fact he says that God wants us to be merciful to others rather than give sacrifices. (Matthew 9:13; 12:7; Mark 12:33)

Read the first two phrases from the prayer thoughtfully. (Matthew 6:9) Here are some questions for your own reflection as you meditate on this part of the prayer.

Am I fearful about approaching God?

Do I sometimes feel that God will not respond to me unless I perform certain acts?

What helps me draw closer to God?

What procedure for prayer have I learned in the past that blocks me from feeling personal with God? What is helpful?

What words in these phrases of the Lord's Prayer help me to draw closer to God?

THE SESSION:

Gathering

Greet the students and give each of them a name tag. Tell them that they are going to learn about the special way that Jesus taught us to pray.

Invite an early student to help you prepare a Celebration Table. To prepare the table, use a small table or card table and cover it with a white tablecloth. In the center place a piece of fabric with the appropriate color, depending on when you teach these sessions. (See the chart for the proper color to use.) Include a candle and a Bible opened to Matthew 6:7. Each session you will add a focal point to the table. For this session place colored crepe paper streamers on the table.

colors that correspond to the christian season:

SEASON	TIME	COLOR	MEANING
Advent	4 Sundays before Christmas	purple/blue	royalty of Christ/hope
Christmas	Christmas Eve until Epiphany	white/gold	purity/royalty
Epiphany	Ordinary* January 6 to Lent	green	growth
Lent	Ash Wednesday to Easter	purple	penitence
Easter	Easter to Pentecost	white	purity
Pentecost	50 days after Easter (some churches continue using Pentecost colors several weeks)	red	fire of Holy Spirit
Ordinary*	Time between Pentecost and Advent	green	growth

* The term "ordinary" means – in order

SUPPLIES:
small table,
white tablecloth,
colored fabric,
candle, Bible,
colored streamers,
long strip of paper
Work puzzle

NOTE 1A:
Hand out
Reproducible 1A
and pencils. Be sure
that the students
understand the
instructions.

Ask a student to prepare to read the closing prayer in your Praise and Prayer Time.

Begin a large wall mounting of the Lord's Prayer by using large strips of paper. Today have early comers help you write the first phrase (Our Father, who art in heaven, hallowed be they name.) on a strip and mount it on the wall.

EXPERIENCE PRAYER:
introduce the Lord's Prayer

Hand out several translations of the Bible and ask the students to find Matthew 6:5-14. Some students may not know how to find the Scripture. Encourage them to use the Table of Contents and explain that the first number is the chapter and the numbers after the colon are the verses you will be reading.

Ask a volunteer to read the passage and ask the others to follow along in their Bibles, noticing how it may be different. After the reading, **ask: How were the words in your Bible different from those that were read? Why do different Bibles use different words for this prayer?**

Say: Matthew's Gospel was translated from Greek. When someone translates something, they use English words that they think mean the same thing as the words in the other language. Different people may translate words differently, particularly when they are translated at different times. Even our English words sometimes change their meanings over the years.

Hand out Reproducible 1B and read the prayer together.

Then ask: How is this different from what we read in the Bible?

Explain that as early as the end of the third century people were using this prayer in their worship services. They found such joy over the words of the prayer that they continued the prayer, using some of the words from 1 Chronicles 29:10-13. Look up that passage and have a volunteer read it.

Read the verses together as a prayer.

CENTER ON THE PHRASE:
introduce the Phrase

Write the first phrase on a long piece of paper or posterboard that is big enough for you to add additional phrases each week. You will do this with different colored markers so that they are recognized by phrases.

Read the phrase together as a group. Then **ask: Who was Jesus praying to when he taught this prayer? Why do you suppose Jesus used the word "Father" in the prayer?**

Accept all answers, and center on the ones connecting God with a loving parent.

Ask: What would the most caring, loving parent you can imagine be like? How is such a loving parent like God? (When there is mention of the parent giving gifts, be sure that the connection with God centers on the gifts of nature, family, etc. that God has given us, not material possessions, such as bicycles, computer games, etc.)

create poem

Say: We are going to create poems about the way that God reminds us of a loving parent. This is a Japanese form of poetry called "Cinquain" (pronounced "sin-cane"). **Hand out Reproducible 1C and be sure that they understand the directions. Allow the students to work in pairs if they like.**

After the poems are completed, ask any students who would like to, to share their poems with the group.

Explore worship

Say: The next part of this first sentence in the prayer uses a word we seldom use today, "hallowed." This shows that we think of God as the most important thing in our lives. It's sort of like seeing God with awe, or with wonder, admiration, or amazement. It says that God is more than we can even imagine! This can also be called worshiping God.

Ask the students to share something that they like about the worship services in your church. After all who wish have shared, **say: When we worship together we call this "corporate worship." Do you know what the word "cooperate" means? Corporate worship means that we worship together, usually meaning that the whole membership of the church is worshiping together. We can also worship in small groups, and sometimes we worship God alone.**

Use a ball of string or yarn to discuss feelings about worship. Stand or sit in a circle, and as you begin, hold on to the end of the string (or wrap it around your finger) and mention some feeling you have about worshiping God. Then ask the students to think of feelings they have. They may repeat something that someone else has said, if they like. When they raise their hands to speak, roll the string ball (or you may throw the ball) to someone across the circle, making a string connection between you and that person. After sharing, that person will hold on to the string and roll/throw the ball to another. As you proceed across the circle, you will create a web with the string. If you are rolling the ball, everyone will need to hold the string high during the rolling; if throwing the ball, hold the string next to the floor. After you have finished, ask everyone to hold onto the string web, whether they contributed or not. Then lift the web high above your heads and simply **pray: We worship you, our God, in many ways. Thank you for being our God. Amen.**

CENTER ON LIFE:
create collage

Using a large piece of paper and crayons, markers, or paints, create a collage of times we worship God. Each person will add a drawing of some time or place where they can feel close to God. Remind the students that we can worship God at any time and in any place that we feel God close to us.

Ask someone to read Genesis 1:26. Remind the students that this verse comes after God created everything else. We were created to be like God, in God's image.

SUPPLIES:
ball of string or yarn

SUPPLIES:
large paper and crayons, markers, or paints

13

Ask: How can we see what God is like? Can we see it in nature? Can we see it in other people?

Say: Think about God as your parent. Parents and children often have similarities. Take a piece of paper and draw a line down the middle. On the left, at the top, write "I am like my parent...." On the right, at the top, write "I am created like God...."

After they have their papers ready, ask them to write words or draw symbols on each side of the paper, showing ways that they are like their parents and created like God.
As they finish,

Say: How does seeing yourself as created by God change your ideas of yourself? How does seeing God as the head of your "family" change the way you would pray to God?

Learn Song: Jim Kilgore

Tell the students that you will use this song to call them together for your Prayer and Praise Time at the end of each session. As they hear the song, they will join in singing and move to the Celebration Table.

Prayer and Praise: w/sing

Call the class to the Celebration Table for Praise and Prayer by singing the song you just learned, "Come! Come! Everybody Worship!" Light the candle and call their attention to the appropriate seasonal color, explaining its meaning. Call their attention to the streamers on the table. **Ask: Why do you suppose we placed this on the table?**

Remind the students that the phrase in the Lord's Prayer, "...hallowed be thy name," refers to worshiping God. **Say: Remember, we can worship God at any time and in many ways. In the Psalms, in the Bible, we read of worshiping God. We will take the streamers and wave them as I read the psalm from the Bible.**

Read Psalm 100 from the Bible or use the boxed translation.

Say: Each session we will have
    someone lead us as we pray. At the end of that per-
    son's prayer, we will all pray the Lord's Prayer together.
Ask the student you assigned earlier to close with the following prayer:

Our God, we thank you that Jesus taught us how to pray. We worship you and thank you for being like a loving parent to us. Amen.

Pray the Lord's Prayer together.

SUPPLIES 1D:
Reproducible 1D

NOTE 1D:
Hand out Reproducible 1D and sing "Come! Come! Everybody Worship!" together

PSALM 100:

Shout praises to the LORD,
everyone on this earth.
Be joyful and sing
as you come in
to worship the LORD!

You know the LORD is God!
He created us,
and we belong to him;
we are his people,
the sheep in his pasture.

Be thankful and praise the LORD
as you enter his temple.
The LORD is good!
His love and faithfulness
will last forever.
    -- Psalm 100
(Contemporary English Version)

Instructions:

Read the paragraphs about prayer. Then find the underlined words in the puzzle below and circle them. The words may be printed horizontally, vertically, or diagonally.

There are many forms of prayer. We might say that prayer is talking with God. Sometimes we talk with God when we are with other people, and sometimes we pray alone.

Sometimes we bow our heads and close our eyes to pray. This may help us concentrate on our prayer. However, we do not need to be in any special position to pray. We can pray as we walk down the street or as we begin to take a test.

Some of the prayers that we say in church were written many years ago by church leaders. These may be called heritage prayers. When we pray these prayers together we are praying with Christians of the past as well as today.

Writing down our thoughts as we pray is called journaling. This helps us think about the prayers more and helps us remember what we have prayed about.

By using the word ACTS we can remember four important parts of prayers:

Adoration — We say how we adore God.
Confession — We tell God we are sorry for what we have done wrong.
Thanksgiving — We thank God for all that is given to us.
Supplication — We recognize our needs and turn them over to God.

```
N O P S N T H N C A H G S E I R R E O R A R O
K O T H A N K S G I V I N G S C N R G I O A V
N I I C A S A C U G E I P P T O O E N C J G O
A R A T I C R T P O S I T I O N I K O E C I S
N A T L A T T G N H K I O R R C T G I R N O D
S G G G S S O S O V O E K I P E A N S S N A O
C G S S I I I T A O O O Y R T N R O S C O S V
P J O U R N A L I N G I A N T T O I E G N H S
T A L K I N G J P K A Y I I O R D E F G R G P
O A T L H O C R T P E A P I N A A K N N N E S
A C R A S A H H I R U G C T N T O A O O T G O
I T P O N N E I O S C S H I F E N I C T R C O
R O O E L L L R H E R I T A G E N K A G O Y O
N G E Y A U O I I I T S N O T C I I O G T A D
S L C C E N A S R H S O N I O L I A I I R K G
N I S A N A N T N I I N I I I A O R C O I O T
```

Words to Find in the Word Find

prayer
talking
concentrate
position
heritage
journaling
Acts
adoration
confession
thanksgiving
supplication

THE LORD'S PRAYER

Our Father, who art in heaven,
hallowed be thy name.

Thy kingdom come, thy will be done
on earth as it is in heaven.

Give us this day our daily bread.

And forgive us our trespasses,
as we forgive those who trespass against us.

And lead us not into temptation,
but deliver us from evil.

For Thine is the kingdom,
and the power, and the glory,
forever. Amen.

REPRODUCIBLE 1C: cinquain Poem

instructions:

Select a subject and write a cinquain (sin cane) poem about it by using the following form and filling in words that express that subject.

Example: Parent, Loves me, Smiling, Providing, Forgiving, Can always be depended, God

LINE 1: A title of one word or one subject.

LINE 2: Two words about the subject (either a phrase or separate words).

LINE 3: Three verbs that denote action. These may end in "ing" or may be phrase of action.

LINE 4: Four words telling about the feeling for line one. May also be a phrase.

LINE 5: One word that means same as first line (or reuse the first word or Amen).

_____

_____   _____

_____   _____   _____

_____   _____   _____   _____

_____

"Come! Come! Everybody Worship"

WORDS and MUSIC: Natalie Sleeth

© 1991 Cokesbury; admin. by The Copyright Co., Nashville, TN

SESSION 2

What does God want Earth to be like, and how do we help make it so?

Thy kingdom come, thy will be done on earth as it is in heaven.

BACKGROUND:

NOTE: Before you begin, read the Introduction, particularly the information on page 6 titled "Teaching These Lessons."

The New Testament, as well as the Old Testament concept of heaven is a physical place. With the mystery of space above the earth, it is quite natural that this was considered the dwelling place of God, the ultimate reign of perfection. The kingdom of heaven was where all that is wrong would be made right—where all of the dreams of a ravished nation would come about. It is the desired "better country" that they hoped to reach away from the disappointments of their earthly predicament. Jesus often spoke of the kingdom, explaining it with parables. He also said in Luke 17:21 that the kingdom is here with us—in our hearts. The people just could not grasp the kingdom as anything other than a physical paradise.

The phrase, "kingdom of heaven" is only found in Matthew's Gospel. Other places in the Bible refer to God's kingdom, and these are considered synonyms. It may be that Matthew preferred to use the term "heaven" instead of "God" because he was writing for the Jewish audience, and the Jewish religion often avoided speaking the name of God. The name, to them, was as holy as God's self. Substitute names were used for God, and one of those was "heaven."

We pray for God's kingdom on earth as in heaven. A king has total control of the kingdom. Do we really want that? Do we want God to have complete control of everything on earth? God could have made us like puppets, and then God would have had complete control. Since, however, God gave us free will, how can God's kingdom come on earth as in heaven? In order for this to happen, and for us to continue to have free will, we must each dedicate our wills to God's will. God's kingdom comes on earth through each and every one of us.

Read this phrase from the prayer thoughtfully. (Matthew 6:10) Here are some questions for your own reflection as you meditate on this part of the prayer.

What will need to happen in order for God's kingdom to take place on earth?

What part do I have in bringing about God's kingdom?

Will the kingdom of God come about if I do nothing?

Do I want God's kingdom to come about through me?

What will this mean to my life?

THE SESSION:
Gathering

Greet the students and, if they do not know each other, give each of them a name tag. Tell them that they are going to learn what Jesus taught us about God's kingdom.

Invite an early student to help you prepare a Celebration Table. (See page 11 for instructions on preparing the table.) For this session place a globe or world map by the candle on the table. Ask a student to prepare to read the closing prayer in your Praise and Prayer Time.

Add to the large wall mounting of the Lord's Prayer by using large strips of paper. Today have early comers help you write the second phrase (Thy kingdom come, thy will be done on earth as it is in heaven.) on a strip and mount it on the wall.

Paraphrase the Lord's Prayer *Group Opening*

Hand out copies of Reproducible 1B (see page 16) and copies of Reproducible 2A. Ask the students to read the paraphrased version of the prayer on Reproducible 2A and use it and the traditional version on Reproducible 1B to create their own paraphrase of the prayer. They may work in pairs if you like. Spend some time sharing the various paraphrased versions in class.

EXPERIENCE PRAYER:
Pray for the World

Ahead of time, clip articles from the paper that tell about negative events that have happened recently in the nation and around the world (robberies, killings, auto accidents, war situations, etc.) As you are looking for these, also cut out clippings of positive events or actions to be used later in the session.

Lay the clippings of negative events out on the floor or a table and ask students to pick one up and read the headlines and beginning paragraph to get a feel for the event. Then put some quiet music on and ask the students to silently pray for the people who were involved in the events recorded in their clipping. Suggest that they pray that God give strength to the victims and for-giveness to those who did wrong.

Take up the clippings to use later.

CENTER ON THE PHRASE:
Learn Definition of "Kingdom"

Hand out several dictionaries and ask students to look up the word "king-dom" and read the definitions to the class. Hand out Bibles and ask students to look up these Scriptures that tell about God's kingdom:

Kingdom as a mustard seed	Mark 4:30-31
Kingdom like yeast	Luke 13:20-21
Kingdom like hidden treasure	Matthew 13:44
Kingdom like a valuable pearl	Matthew 13:45-46
Kingdom is here with you	Luke 17:20-21

Ask: What have you learned about God's kingdom from reading the dictionary definitions and the Scripture passages?

Learn about God's Will

They may give such answers as these:
God's kingdom is where God rules.
God's kingdom grows when the right circumstances are there.
God's kingdom can expand.
God's kingdom is coming about now.
God's kingdom is more important than anything else in the world.

SUPPLIES:
dictionaries,
Bibles

Say: The section of the Lord's Prayer that we are centering on today asks that God's will be done on earth as well as in heaven. Many people have different ideas about the will of God. When have you heard people say something about the will of God, and what did they say?

After several have shared their experiences, hand out Reproducible 2B and say: **During a war in England, people were asking if all of the killing was really what God willed or wanted to happen. This tells how one pastor answered the people's questions.**

Review the information on the reproducible and answer any questions that might arise.

CENTER ON LIFE:
Review Newspaper Clippings

Ahead of time cut clippings from the newspaper and/or magazines that illustrate the three wills of God (see Reproducible 2B). These will include positive and negative actions by people and feature articles that tell about the world or ways that people care for the earth. Be sure that there are at least a couple of articles for each of the three "Wills" of God. The intentional will would be articles where a good action took place; circumstantial will would be negative actions; ultimate will would be articles where something bad happened, but good finally came about.

SUPPLIES:
Reproducible 2B

Hand out the newspaper clippings used earlier in the session and any additional clippings you brought telling of positive events and actions. Assign three sections of the room (Intentional Will, Circumstantial Will, Ultimate Will), and have the students move to the section that their article reflects. They may need to review Reproducible 2B as they decide on the section. The students will talk in their groups and decide on one article among them that illustrates their assigned "will." Then bring the students back together and ask each group to share their chosen article. When the circumstantial will article is shared, ask what could happen to make that circumstance into an ultimate will of God.

Work Puzzle

Hand out Reproducible 2C and pencils and be sure that the students understand the directions. Answers to crossword:

Plan Project

Talk together about some sort of mission project that your class can work on during the remainder of the study. Remind them that helping others is a way to help God's kingdom to come on earth, as it is in heaven. Several suggestions are listed. Consult your pastor or someone on your Mission Committee for additional suggestions.

Jim

Learn Song

Hand out Reproducible 2D and learn the song, "Wisely Made!" **Say: This song reminds us that each and every thing that God made was made wisely and for a purpose. We are all a part of God's kingdom.**

After learning the song, sing it as a prayer.

❑ Collect food for a food pantry.
❑ Visit in an extended care home.
❑ Bring socks, mittens, or caps for deprived children.
❑ Arrange to glean fruits or vegetables at the end of a picking season. Give them to a soup kitchen.
❑ Make sandwiches and/or serve at a soup kitchen.
❑ Collect school supplies for a mission school
❑ Clean the yard of an elderly person in your church or community.
❑ Pick up litter in a park or roadside. (If on a roadside, take caution by wearing reflective vests.)

PRAYER AND PRAISE:

Call the class to the Celebration Table for Praise and Prayer by singing "Come! Come! Everybody Worship!" Light the candle and call their attention to the appropriate seasonal color, reminding them of its meaning. Call their attention to the globe or world map on the table.
Ask: Why do you suppose we placed this on the table?

Ask: What are some ways that you can help to bring God's kingdom about during this next week?

Ask the student you assigned earlier to close with the boxed prayer and remind the class that they will pray the Lord's Prayer at the close of the student's prayer.

Pray the Lord's Prayer together.

PRAYER:
Our God, we know that your kingdom is a good one. We want to help your kingdom to come and for your will to be done. Amen.

---

instructions:

Use the space on the right side of the page to write your own version
of the Lord's Prayer. Use words that are natural to you.

Our Parent God,

the source of love throughout
    the universe.

We shout praises of joy to you, calling
    your name holy!

May your justice be among all the
    people of the earth,

and your loving will be done by all
    persons, as you would have it.

Give us bread each day so that we can
    share it with others.

Forgive us when we fail to love
    and care for each other.

We will try to live out our forgiveness
    for those who hurt us.

Give us strength to live under the
    temptations that come our way.

Free us from the many evil occasions
    in this world.

For you are the greatest, and
    your love is for now and forever.

Amen.

Then God said, "Let us make humankind in our image, according to our likeness; and let them have dominion over the fish of the sea, and over the birds of the air, and over the cattle, and over all the wild animals of the earth, and over every creeping thing that creeps upon the earth." (Genesis 1:26)

We were created in the image of God. That means that we have the ability to decide on things. God did not make us like puppets. We can decide to do what God wants us to do, or we can decide not to. But what is it that God wants? What is the will of God?

During a war in England, there were many innocent people being killed—adults and children alike. Many people asked if the killings were what God wanted. A preacher in London preached several sermons that helped the people understand God's will. This is a summary of what he said.

Intentional Will – This is the way that God intended (planned) the world to be from the beginning. God created us all and set the world up so that everyone would have enough to eat and we would be loving and caring for each other and live happy lives.

Circumstantial Will – God also intended (planned) for us to be free to choose what we want to do. In those situations (circumstances) we can choose to do what is best for God's world and for God's people, or we can choose not to do the right thing. Sometimes we may not even understand and may choose wrong. But because God decided to give us a choice, in these circumstances it is God's will and God allows it to happen.

Ultimate Will – However, God can use even bad choices and make things work out for the good. The word "ultimate" means final. If we listen to God and try to continue to do what God wants us to do, God can make the world good for all of us, even after bad things happen.

instructions:
God's World

God has a plan for our world and for how we can live together peacefully. Read the statements about God's plan below and fill the missing words into the crossword puzzle.

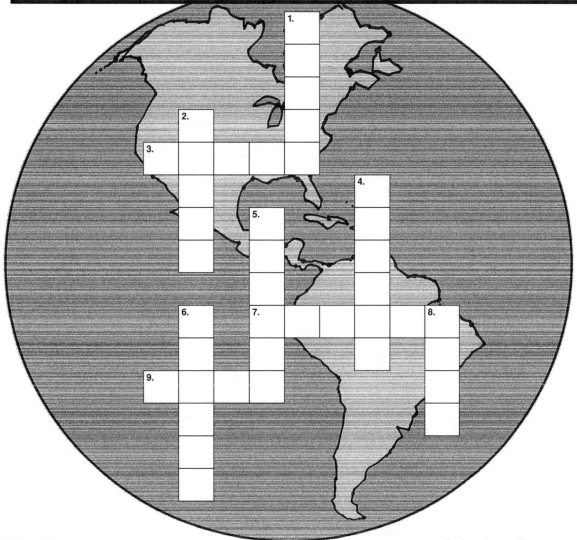

ACROSS

3. When people disagree they will learn to live together in _ _ _ _ _.
7. There will be enough trees and other _ _ _ _ _ _ to make oxygen for people to breathe.
9. People will _ _ _ _ each other instead of hate.

DOWN

1. People will _ _ _ _ _ food with others so that everyone has enough to eat.
2. People will have enough _ _ _ _ _ to drink and not waste it.

4. Grasses and shrubs will grow on hillsides so that the _ _ _ _ _ _ won't wash away.
5. Everyone will have _ _ _ _ _ _ who love and care for them.
6. We will learn about weather so that we can protect ourselves from _ _ _ _ _ _ and other natural disasters.
8. When people are _ _ _ _, they will have a doctor to help them get well.

"Wisely Made"

WORDS: James Ritchie (refrain adapted from Psalm 104:24, *Good News Bible*)
MUSIC: James Ritchie
ARRANGEMENT: Timothy Edmonds
Refrain © 1989 Graded Press; words and music stanzas 1, 2, 3 © 1990 James Ritchie

SESSION 3

What should we ask God for and why?

Give us this day our daily bread.

BACKGROUND:

This is perhaps the most personal part of the prayer, and we often rush past it, thinking it's just asking for food. This phrase does indicate that God cares about our welfare. God is concerned with the details of our lives. Jesus understood God as a personal God, one who is involved in our lives in every way, even down to the routine job of providing food for the table.

Notice, however, that this phrase speaks of "daily" bread. This reminds us of the Hebrews gathering manna each day in the wilderness. God's instruction to them was to gather only what they needed for that day, because any excess would go bad on them, and it did. If we eat in excess, taking in more than is needed, it simply goes to fat, which can be harmful to our bodies. Sleep is something like that too. They tell us that we cannot store up sleep ahead of time. We can sleep well and be rested for a time without sleep, but we can't store it up ahead. We can make up for the loss of sleep afterwards. We cannot store up what we need from God. It is something that is necessary daily. Our physical nourishment and our spiritual nourishment both must be taken in daily.

Another word in this phrase that we often miss is the word "our." Jesus did not tell us to pray, "Give me this day my daily bread." Jesus was very definite in the use of the plural pronoun. God created us in community, and what God gives must be shared by all. Our planet provides enough food to feed everyone, and there is enough energy to keep us all warm and enough wealth for everyone to have the basic needs met. But we must share our abundance for this to happen. This is a different way of living that Jesus is calling us to. Our abundance can be the answer to the prayers of others who are not as fortunate as we.

Notice that this is the only phrase in the prayer that asks specifically for material things. How often we pray for specifics and then feel something is wrong when the prayers are not answered in the manner we had hoped. For certain, those around the world who go to bed hungry each night are praying for food, and relatives of the dying continue to pray for physical healing as they stand by their bedsides. But the hungry aren't fed and the sick aren't healed miraculously. This does not mean that we should stop asking, because asking shows that we trust in God. Asking shows that our relationship with God goes beyond a "Santa" God.

As you reread this phrase from the prayer, reflect on these questions:

When did you last ask for something in a prayer? How did you feel about asking?

Did you receive it? How did you feel then?

How do you see the gifts that you receive in relation to others in need?

NOTE:
Before you begin, read the introduction, particularly the information on page 6 titled "Teaching These Lessons."

How are those gifts claimed by God?

Do you know anyone personally who is in need of food, clothing, medical care, or other necessities of life?

What difference would knowing such a person make in your attitude about your own wealth?

When has God met a need of yours through someone else?

Have you thanked God for those persons?

THE SESSION:
Gathering

Greet the students and, if they do not know each other, give each of them a name tag. Tell them that they are going to learn what Jesus taught us about asking God for things.

Invite an early student to help you prepare a Celebration Table. (See page 11 for instructions on preparing the table.) For this session place a loaf of bread by the candle on the table.

Ask a student to prepare to read the closing prayer in your Praise and Prayer Time.

Add to the large wall mounting of the Lord's Prayer by using large strips of paper. Today have early comers help you write the third phrase (Give us this day our daily bread.) on a strip and mount it on the wall.

Graffiti Wall

Place a large piece of paper on the wall and label it "Everyone has a right to _____." As students enter, ask them to use crayons to write words or draw symbols that complete the sentence. These may be items such as food, water, basic clothing, medicine, love, peace, etc. They may also include concepts such as a right to ask questions, to free speech, to be heard, etc. (Note: Markers may be used, but be sure that markers do not bleed through onto the wall.)

EXPERIENCE PRAYER:
Learn the Prayer

An easy way to help students learn the Lord's Prayer is to use a pocket chart. The pocket chart is made by taking posterboard and creating long pockets along the board with folded strips of long paper. Fold the long strips of paper in half lengthwise. Placing the strips horizontally on the board with the crease facing down, space them evenly down the posterboard, taping the strips across the bottom and folding the ends around the edges of the posterboard, taping them to secure.

Write the words or phrases of the prayer at the top of 3" x 5" cards, and place them in order in the pockets. Read the prayer together. Then in subsequent readings, randomly remove one of the cards. (Note: If your class is small, you can create the same learning experience by simply placing the cards, face up, on the floor or table and removing the cards as you learn the prayer.)

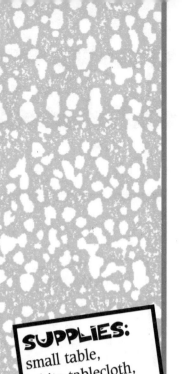

SUPPLIES:
small table,
white tablecloth,
colored fabric,
candle,
Bible,
loaf of bread,
long strip of paper

SUPPLIES:
large paper, crayons

SUPPLIES:
1 piece of posterboard or heavy cardboard (22"x 28"); 4 three-inch strips of paper (such as freezer or shelf paper), each 30 inches long; transparent tape; index cards (same number as there are words or phrases)

CENTER ON THE PHRASE:
Review Products

Give each student copies of Reproducible 3A and 3B and a pencil. Ask them to look at the picture and fill in the blanks on the other page.

After they have completed the pages, **ask: What did you learn that you didn't know about the things that we use daily?**

After they answer, **say: In Jesus' prayer he taught us to ask for our "daily bread." This is a way of saying that we need to only expect the necessary things in life. What items in the picture are necessities and what are "niceities"—things that are nice to have but not necessary?**

SUPPLIES:
Reproducibles 3A and 3B, pencils

CENTER ON LIFE:
Discuss Necessities and Niceities

Ahead of time collect an assortment of items from your home that represent the necessities of life and the "niceities"—things that are nice to have but not necessary. Be sure to include food items, medicine, toothpaste, water, and basic clothing items as necessities. You might also include a heart to represent love as a necessity. For "niceities" include computer games, any current "fad" items, can of soda, candy bar, etc. Other items—such as car keys, book bags, warm coat, etc.—may be discussed, because in some situations each may be a necessity and in other situations they may be niceities.

Spread the items out on the floor or a table and ask students to select an item and tell why they think it is a necessity or a niceity.

Read together the phrase from the Lord's Prayer and **ask: How does our discussion about necessities and niceities relate to this phrase?** They may answer that we pray for our daily needs, not just anything that we want. Point out that the prayer also uses the plural pronoun "us," which includes everyone in the world.

Work Maze Puzzle

Hand out Reproducible 3C and pencils and give the students time to find their way through the maze. After they have finished, **say: Look at the words at places in the puzzle. What do you notice about these words and where they are placed in the puzzle?** (*The ones that you cross to follow the right path are necessities, and the ones that lead to dead ends are "niceities."*) **Ask: What does this say about what is important for us to pray for? Does this mean that God doesn't want us to have nice things?**

SUPPLIES 3C:
Reproducible 3C, pencils

Play Game

Say: This game is played something like "Fruit Basket Turn Over." I will give you names of things that are necessities, things that everyone needs in order to live as God wants us to live. We will sit in a circle with one less chair than there are players. "It" will stand in the middle of the circle and call two of the "necessities." The two of you with those names will exchange places while "It" tries to get a seat.

The person left standing then becomes "It." If "All over the world!" is called, then everyone changes places. Assign the boxed names to the players and write the names on a chalk board or large paper for "It" to be able to see:

food _____
water _____
clean air _____
clothing _____
house _____
love _____

Supplies 3D:
Reproducible 3 D

Learn Song

Hand out Reproducible 3D and learn the song, "God Made the Earth." **Say: God provided everything on the earth and all that we need daily. We can thank God in a prayer song.** After learning the song, sing it as a prayer.

PRAYER AND PRAISE:

Call the class to the Celebration Table for Praise and Prayer by singing "Come! Come! Everybody Worship!" Light the candle and call their attention to the appropriate seasonal color, reminding them of its meaning. Call their attention to the bread on the table. **Ask: Why do you suppose we placed this on the table?**

Call attention to the graffiti wall that you created at the beginning of the session. Review the comments and drawings on the paper. **Ask: Considering what we've learned today, do these statements still hold true? How do they relate to the words in the phrase that we are studying today?**

PRAYER

Our God, we sometimes want things because it is popular to have them. Too often we forget about others who don't even have the basic necessities of life. Help us to remember what is important. Amen.

Ask the student you assigned earlier to close with the boxed prayer.

Pray the Lord's Prayer together.

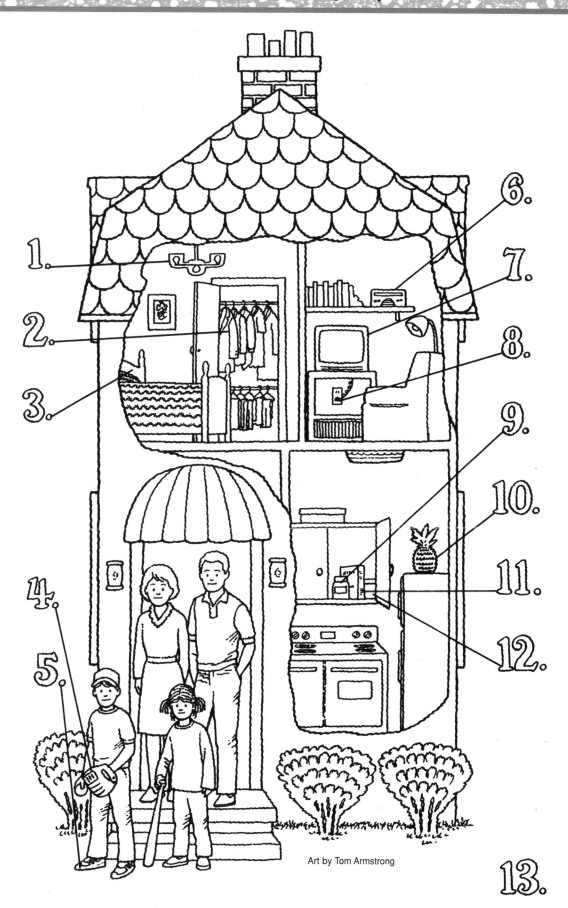

1.
2.
3.
4.
5.
6.
7.
8.
9.
10.
11.
12.
13.

Art by Tom Armstrong

From *Helping Children Care for God's People* by Delia Halverson, Copyright © 1994 by Abingdon Press.

1. Filament for light from Bolivia.   How many lights do you have in your house? _____   *A U.S. child will use 30 to 50 times more goods in a lifetime than one born in Bolivia's poor section.*   What did you buy this year that you no longer use?_____   Why don't you use it anymore?

_____

2. Clothing from Costa Rica. How many shirts do you have?_____   *Workers in Costa Rica earn less than 40 cents an hour.*   What do you do with the clothing you outgrow?_____

3. Teak furniture from Honduras. What furniture do you have that is made of teak?_____   *About 75 percent of the people in Honduras live in small rural villages and earn about $6.00 a month.*   What did you pay for your last toy?_____

4. Baseball and glove from Haiti.   Do you have a baseball and glove?_____   *In a Haitian village of 6,000 people, there usually are only two water taps. One out of every five babies born in Haiti dies before its second birthday.*   How many children do you know under two?_____

5. Rubber in sneakers from Thailand.   How many pairs of sneakers are there in your house?_____   *Most people in Thailand make $528 a year, or $10.15 a week.*   How much allowance do you get a week, and how do you spend it?

_____

6. Radio assembled in Taiwan.   How many radios does your family own?_____   *Workers in Taiwan earn less than 25 cents an hour.*   What did you last spend 25 cents on?_____

7. Parts of the television come from Burundi.   How many televisions do you have?_____   *People in Burundi seldom live to be older than 42 years.*   Do you know anyone who is about 42?_____

8. Electricity made from coal mined in Clear Fork Valley, Kentucky.   How many electrical outlets are in your house?_____   *Two-thirds of the houses in Clear Fork Valley do not have flush toilets.*   How many flush toilets do you have in your house?_____

9. Coffee from Guatemala.   Who in your house drinks coffee?_____   *Two out of every three people in Guatemala make only $42.00 a year.*   What have you bought or been given that costs about $42.00?_____

10. Pineapples from the Philippines.   Do you eat pineapples or drink the juice?_____
Half of the children in the Philippines under four years of age are ill because they do not get enough protein.   Who do you know that is under four years of age?_____

11. Cocoa and fish from Ecuador.   When do you enjoy cocoa?_____
Do you ever have tuna fish sandwiches for lunch?_____   *In Equador, 60 percent of the children do not have enough to eat to keep them healthy.*   What was the longest time you went without food, and how did it feel?_____

12. Sugar from the Dominican Republic.   What foods that you like best contain sugar?_____
Only 30 percent of the children in Dominican Republic ever live to be five years old.   Who do you know that is five?_____

13. Other common items supplied by poor countries: tea from Bangladesh, copper wiring from Chile, aluminum from Jamaica, tin from Malaysia, dog food made of fishmeal from Peru, cork (for bulletin board) from Algeria, natural gas from Mexico

instructions:

What's Important?
Find your way out of the maze following "**The way out.**"

The way out
vegetables
bread
clean water
love
milk
clothing
housing
medicine

Dead end
television
computer game
DVD
candy
soda
video
Disney world trip
guitar

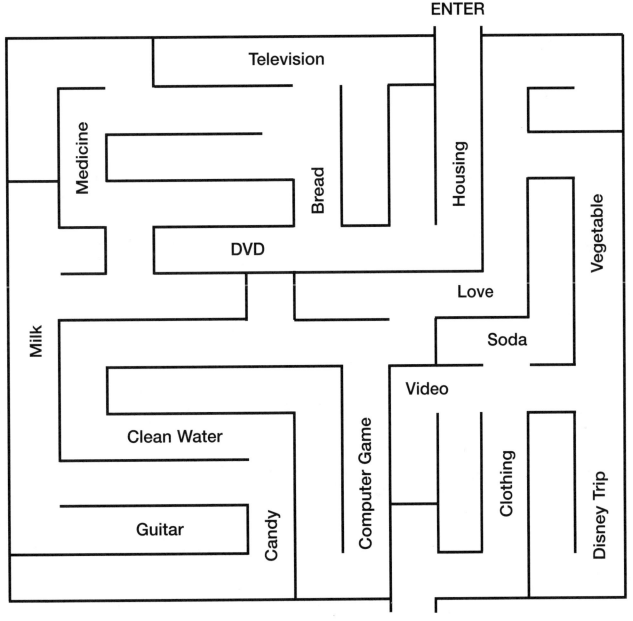

GIVE US THIS DAY, OUR DAILY BREAD

"God Made the Earth"

1. God made the earth, God made the sea, all liv-ing things made for you and me. Care for God's good earth each day, ___
2. God made the day, God made the night, sun, moon, and stars giv-ing us great light. Shin-ing on the earth so fair which

give your thanks in ev-ery way. } God made the earth, God saw that it was good.
God has left ___ to our care.

Optional Handbells or Glockenspiel

Last time

Suggestions for singing:
    melody and bell ostinato only
    melody, accompaniment, and bells
    melody and accompaniment

WORDS and MUSIC: Susan Eltringham, based on Genesis 1:10
© 1993 Abingdon Press

SESSION 4

What is sin and how do we ask for forgiveness and forgive others?

And forgive us our trespasses, as we forgive those who trespass against us.

NOTE:
Before you begin, read the introduction, particularly the information on page 6 titled "Teaching These Lessons."

BACKGROUND:

There are several ways of saying this phrase. The most common one is to use the word "trespass." This comes from the King James Version of the Bible, which was the common one used for so many years that it continues to be the favored wording for this phrase. However, if your church uses "debts" or "sins," adjust the language for your teaching.

This part of the prayer really gets personal—almost too personal. If we pray this prayer with understanding and with intention, then we are digging into our less-than-perfect selves. Most of us haven't committed serious sins, but then who are we to decide just what is "serious" and what isn't? Any time we've acted in a way that breaks our relationship with God, we need forgiveness. But, you ask, why should we ask for forgiveness when God, who knows everything, knows that we are sorry? Acknowledgment clears the way to acceptance of that forgiveness and mends the relationship with God.

Even after we have asked God to forgive us, we often continue to berate ourselves for our failures. We feel so strongly that we are expected to be perfect that it continues to rest on our shoulders. Jesus used an example of the yoke and the oxen here. This has two implications. First, any pull of the plow is easier with two yoked together than with one. We don't have to go it alone. Forgiveness takes the load off our shoulders. The other implication is that Jesus, as the lead or mature oxen, will teach us the way. This he did with the Lord's Prayer. Jesus assured us that we are forgiven.

Now the prayer goes on beyond our own forgiveness. The prayer is no longer about my receiving, but the conditions turn to my giving—my giving forgiveness. Often we think that when we forgive, we dilute the seriousness of the wrong that others did. Forgiving, however, does the opposite. If we forgive, we acknowledge that the act was wrong. We say "What you did hurt me, and it is not right before God." Forgiveness also releases the bond of hatred that keeps us from moving forward. We are free from the energy-draining effort of hatred. Forgiving others enables us to accept the forgiveness of God.

As we forgive, and as God forgives us, we can put the past behind us and move forward. Otherwise, we are always chained to the past.

As you reread this phrase from the prayer, reflect on these questions:

If Paul hadn't forgiven himself for what he had done to the Christians, would his ministry and writings have been as effective?

35

If Joseph hadn't forgiven his brothers for selling him into slavery, would he have been able to function as well in the pharaoh's court and become a leader who could help his family later?

How heavily do you suppose the burden of guilt hung over Peter's head as he recalled denying that he knew Jesus? How did his asking for and accepting God's forgiveness make a difference in his ministry?

Which is harder, to forgive yourself or to forgive others?

What act against you have you found the hardest to forgive? Why?

How did you feel after you asked someone to forgive you? If you have never asked anyone for forgiveness, why?

How hard is it to be gracious to someone who asks for your forgiveness?

Who has personified God's graciousness in forgiveness? What about that person would you like to make a part of you?

THE SESSION:
Gathering

Greet the students and, if they do not know each other, give each of them a name tag. Tell them that they are going to learn what Jesus taught us about asking for forgiveness.

Invite an early student to help you prepare a Celebration Table. (See page 11 for instructions on preparing the table.) For this session place a bowl with water by the candle on the table.

Ask a student to prepare to read the closing prayer in your Praise and Prayer Time.

Add to the large wall mounting of the Lord's Prayer by using large strips of paper. Today have early comers help you write the fourth phrase (And forgive us our trespasses, as we forgive those who trespass against us.) on a strip and mount it on the wall.

EXPERIENCE PRAYER:
Learn Motions to the Lord's Prayer

Lead the class in saying the Lord's Prayer creating your own motions. After learning the motions and using them with spoken prayer, if you have a recording of a musical version of the Lord's Prayer, use the motions to the music.

CENTER ON THE PHRASE:
Check Definitions

Hand out dictionaries and ask the students to look up these words: debt, sin, trespass. Read the definitions out loud and **ask: What do these words have in common?**

SUPPLIES:
small table, white tablecloth, colored fabric, candle, Bible, bowl with water, long strip of paper

NOTE:
If your church uses the word "sin" or "debts" and "debtors", use those words in the phrase.

Read today's phrase from the Lord's Prayer together. Tell them that sometimes when we pray the Lord's Prayer we use the word "trespass," and sometimes we use the words "debt" or "sin."

Say: Let's think for a moment about the word "debt." A debt is something that we owe. We owe the store money when we buy something. Sometimes we do something for someone because we want them to be in "debt" to us—we say "You owe me one!" When Jesus says to forgive others their debts, what does that say about how we should treat others?

Why Ask?

Hand out Reproducible 4A and assign parts. After the play reading at the top of the page, divide the class into groups of twos or threes to discuss the questions at the bottom. Tell them to write their own thoughts after their discussion and that there are no right or wrong answers to the questions.

Bring the class back together and allow anyone to share their answers if they like. After those who wish have shared, ask what the phrase of the Lord's Prayer that you are studying today has to do with the questions you've just discussed.

CENTER ON LIFE:
Dialing Debtless Actions Puzzle

Hand out Reproducible 4B and pencils. Be sure that the students understand the directions.

jump forward two jumps
walk toward me backward three steps
take four steps forward
hop forward one hop

Forgiveness Game

Assign one person to be the "Forgiver" and the other players line up across one end of the room. The Forgiver is at the opposite side of the room. The Forgiver will call a person's name and tell him or her to do various things while moving forward, such as: (Look in box.)

The person whose name is called, before making a move, must say "Will you forgive me?" The Forgiver will say "You are forgiven," and the person can move. If the person does not ask to be forgiven, then he or she must move backward the number of steps/hops/jumps that they would have moved forward. Continue the game until everyone has progressed to the other side of the room. When players get to the other side of the room, they will cheer the remaining players on as they finish.

After the game is finished, **ask: How did it feel to have to ask for forgiveness? How did it feel when you forgot to ask for forgiveness? How did it feel when you got in the habit of asking for forgiveness?**

Learn of the Holy Spirit

Hand out Reproducible 4C and **say: Look at this drawing. What do you see? (If you concentrate on the white areas, you see a question mark. If**

SUPPLIES 4A:
Reproducible 4A, pencils

SUPPLIES 4B:
Reproducible 4B, pencils

37

you concentrate on the dark areas you see a dove.)

Ask a student to read Matthew 3:13-17. **Say: When we have questions about forgiveness and about living so that we don't commit sins, we can know that the Holy Spirit can help us. Because of this Scripture, we Christians use the dove as a symbol for the Holy Spirit.**

Learn Song

Hand out Reproducible 4D and learn the song, "Come Holy Spirit, Heavenly Dove." **Say: The way that God helps us know how to act is sometimes called the Holy Spirit, and a symbol that we use for the Holy Spirit is the dove.** After learning the song, sing it as a prayer.

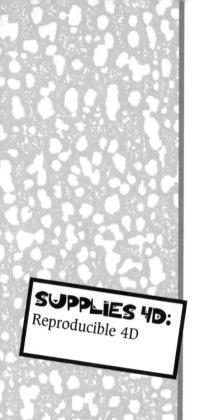

SUPPLIES 4D:
Reproducible 4D

Prayer and Praise

Call the class to the Celebration Table for Praise and Prayer by singing "Come! Come! Everybody Worship!" Light the candle and call their attention to the appropriate seasonal color, reminding them of its meaning. Call their attention to the bowl of water on the table. **Ask: Why do you suppose we placed this on the table?**

After several have responded, **say: We are going to have a blessing of forgiveness as we close, using the water symbolically.**

Ask everyone to stand in a circle around the Celebration Table. Then ask them to each think about something that they feel they need to have God forgive. They will not say what it is out loud, but just think about it during the blessing.

Tell the students that you will begin, and then everyone will take a turn assuring each other of their forgiveness. Take the bowl of water from the table and **Say: Let us pray together for forgiveness, using the words from the Lord's Prayer.**

Go to one student and dip your hand in the water and brush water across the student's forehead, **saying: As water washes us clean, remember that God forgives our sins.** Give the bowl to that student who will do the same to the person by him or her, and continue around the circle. Ask the last student to assure you of your forgiveness.

After all have been reminded of forgiveness, ask the student you assigned earlier to close with the boxed prayer.

Pray the Lord's Prayer together.

PRAYER:
Forgive us our trespasses (sins) as we forgive those who trespass against us.
Pray together, as a group, " - forgive us our sins as we forgive those who sin against us."

PRAYER:
Our Forgiving God, we are sometimes afraid to ask for forgiveness and to give forgiveness to others. Help us to remember that Jesus taught us about forgiveness in his prayer. Amen.

NARRATOR: Myrna and Kylie were friends. They had known each other since they were babies. People sometimes said that they knew what each other was thinking. They often finished each other's sentences. One day these good friends did get into a disagreement.

MYRNA: I don't think you should wear your hair that way. It looks strange! It makes you look like an old lady.

KYLIE: That's not very nice, you calling me an old lady! I saw this hair style in the latest magazine.

MYRNA: I don't care where you saw it, it still makes you look like an old lady.

KYLIE: Fine friend you are! Just don't bother to talk to me if that's the way you feel.

NARRATOR: The girls spent several miserable days not talking to each other. Kylie knew that Myrna didn't mean to be hateful when she made the remarks. But she still refused to talk with her. Myrna was sorry for what she had said. Myrna didn't want to say she was sorry for the way she acted because she was sure that since they had been such close friends Kylie would know that she was sorry. Why couldn't they be friends without Myrna having to ask Kylie to forgive her?

What do you think? _____

_____

_____

Why should Myrna tell Kylie she is sorry even though Kylie knew it anyway?

_____

_____

What difference will it make in the girls' relationship if Myrna asks Kylie to forgive her? _____

_____

_____

Why should we ask God to forgive us when God already knows that we are sorry?

_____

_____

What difference will it make in our relationship with God if we ask for forgiveness? _____

_____

instructions:

Sometimes we may do an act of kindness for someone simply because we want that person to be "in debt" to us. We may tell that person, "You owe me one!"

In Jesus' prayer he told us to forgive others. Turning the situation around, we can do kind acts for others without expecting anything in return. We can even do it in secret so that the person doesn't know who did it. Solve the puzzle below to discover kind acts you may do without expecting anything in return.

Look at each set of numbers. The first number shows which button to find. The second number shows which one of the letters on that button to choose for the code. (Hint: 7-3 means to look for button "7." Then choose the letter "R" and write it on the line above 7-3. A slash (/) will be between words.

Cell Phone

2=A,B,C
3=D,E,F
4=G,H,I
5=J,K,L
6=M,N,O
7=P,Q,R
8=S,T,U,V
9=W,X,Y,Z

2-1 6-2 3-1 / 3-3 6-3 7-3 4-1 4-3 8-4 3-2 / 8-3 8-1/

6-3 8-3 7-3 / 8-2 7-3 3-2 8-1 7-1 2-1 8-1 8-1 3-2 8-1 /

2-1 8-1 / 9-1 3-2 / 3-3 6-3 7-3 4-1 4-3 8-4 3-2 /

8-2 4-2 6-3 8-1 3-2 / 9-1 4-2 6-3 /

8-2 7-3 3-2 8-1 7-1 2-1 8-1 8-1 /

2-1 4-1 2-1 4-3 6-2 8-1 8-2 / 8-2 8-1

WHAT DOES THE PUZZLE SAY?

_____

_____

_____

_____

_____

_____

_____

_____

instructions:

Ask a student to read Matthew 3:13-17. **Say: When we have questions about forgiveness and about living so that we don't commit sins, we can know that Jesus sent the Holy Spirit to help us. Because of this Scripture, we Christians use the dove as a symbol for the Holy Spirit.**

By focusing on the light area or the dark area you will see either a question mark or a dove.

"Come, Holy Spirit, Heavenly Dove"

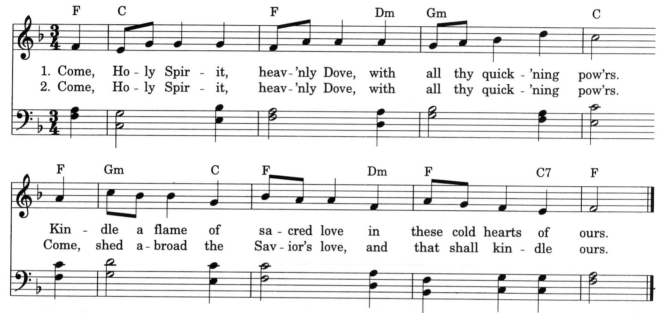

WORDS: Isaac Watts
MUSIC: USA campmeeting melody

SESSION 5

How do we follow God's direction in our lives?

And lead us not into temptation, but deliver us from evil.

BACKGROUND:

This phrase has often caused people to believe that God will test us with temptations. James 1:13 tells us, that God does not "lead us" into temptation. It is actually evil that tempts us. We need to remember that Matthew's Gospel was written in Greek and sometimes the translation comes through in different ways. The recent Contemporary English Version of this verse reads: "Keep us from being tempted." and the J. B. Phillips version reads: "Keep us clear of temptation, and save us from evil." This phrase reminds us that even though there are times when we don't want to do the right things, God is with us helping us overcome that negative attitude.

In Matthew we read that Jesus was tempted. (Matthew 4:1-11) This was just prior to his beginning his ministry, and the human aspect of Jesus must have triggered ways to bring people around to his understanding of God.

(1) Jesus was hungry, and he thought of the many hungry people in the world. If Jesus miraculously fed them all then surely people would take notice and turn to God.

(2) With the power to forego injury, Jesus could have jumped from the highest point of the Temple, which represented the ultimate in the Hebrew faith. Such a display of power would have made a difference in his reception.

(3) Jesus knew that the Hebrews were looking for a leader who would take over their world politically and crush their oppressors. But this would require change by force and not necessarily a change in the heart.

All of these alternatives Jesus considered and rejected. Instead he set about selecting twelve diverse men whom he could work with closely. These men, and the other followers of Jesus, would have a change of heart and go about changing the hearts of people around the world. The change would happen in their hearts instead of by some outward power.

If we recognize Jesus as "God with skin on," then we can know that God has gone through the struggles of temptation. We are better able to relate to a God who understands because of experience. Jesus must have shared these experiences with his disciples in their training, or we would not have a record of this in the Bible.

NOTE:
Before you begin, read the introduction, particularly the information on page 6 titled "Teaching These Lessons."

As you reread this phrase from the prayer, reflect on these questions:

When have you done something that you later regretted or wished you could redo differently? How can you talk to God about these situations?

When have you struggled between something that you wanted and what you believed that God wanted of you? What has helped you choose God's way?

What can you do to remind yourself to pause and turn to God before you act in a manner that is ungodly?

How can Jesus' struggle with temptation make a difference in your own struggles?

Whom do you know who is struggling with a temptation that is not God's way? How can you let that person know that you are praying for him or her?

THE SESSION:
Gathering

Greet the students and, if they do not know each other, give each of them a name tag. Tell them that they are going to learn what Jesus taught us about asking God for things.

Invite an early student to help you prepare a Celebration Table. (See page 11 for instructions on preparing the table.) For this session place a sign with a large red circle and slash on it by the candle on the table. The red circle and slash is the symbol used on roadsides and public places to indicate that certain actions are not allowed.

Ask a student to prepare to read the closing prayer in your Praise and Prayer Time.

Add to the large wall mounting of the Lord's Prayer by using large strips of paper. Today have early comers help you write the fifth phrase (And lead us not into temptation, but deliver us from evil.) on a strip and mount it on the wall.

SUPPLIES:
small table,
white tablecloth,
colored fabric,
candle,
Bible,
sign with red circle and slash,
long strip of paper

Explore Temptation

Hand out Bibles and ask students to work together in pairs to find the Scriptures listed. They will read the Scripture and be prepared to tell the class about it.

Matthew 4:8-10
Romans 7:18-24
1 Corinthians 10:12-13
Hebrews 2:1-8
Hebrews 4:13-16
James 1:13-14

Experience Prayer

Hand out Reproducible 5A and pencils. Explain that you will read together each phrase of the Lord's Prayer as it is printed on the reproducible. Between each phrase you will pause and give everyone opportunity to write his or her own prayer on the spaces below the phrase. When they have completed their prayers, suggest that they take them home and pray their prayers during the week.

CENTER ON THE PHRASE:
Explore Temptation

Ask a student to read the definition of the word "tempt" from the dictionary. Then ask the students to share what they learned about temptation when they read the passages from the Bible. As they share, stress the fact that God does not tempt us, but God helps us overcome the evil that tempts us. Explain that sometimes in translation the exact meaning of a phrase doesn't come across. Share the wording of this phrase from the Contemporary English Version of the Bible: "Keep us from being tempted and protect us from evil."

Create Breath Prayer

Hand out Reproducible 5B and pencils. Tell the students that they will create a prayer that will help them when they are tempted to do something that they shouldn't. A breath prayer is a prayer that is short enough to be said in one breath.

Put some calming music on as they work. Then when everyone is finished, ask that they all sit in silence for a few moments and everyone breathe and say their breath prayer in their minds. Lead them in relaxing by saying the following: **Close your eyes and slowly breathe in and out. Breathe in (pause) Breathe out. (pause) Breathe in. (pause) Breathe out. (pause) Now continue to breathe in and out at that pace and silently say your breath prayer each time you breathe in or out.**

Afterwards encourage them to take their breath prayers home and use them often during the day.

CENTER ON LIFE:
Put Down Put-Downs

Put-downs are common for middle and older elementary children. It can become a game to see who can say the most hurting remarks to or about someone else. They usually say these remarks without even thinking about how they affect the other person. This exercise will help the students realize the results of their put-downs and will remind them that God will help them overcome the temptations to use put-downs.

Ahead of time, draw a large image of a person (in gingerbread man form) on a paper or tag board and cut it out.

Sit together in a circle and **ask: What is a "put-down"?**
Holding the paper "person," **say: I want each of you to think of some put-down that has been said to you or that you've heard someone say to another person. I am going to pass this paper person around the circle, and I'd like for each of you to tell us the put-down that you thought of, and at the same time tear a piece off this paper person.**

Begin by sharing one yourself and tearing an appropriate size piece. If you have a large group, tear off a smaller piece. If your group is very small, you may pass the paper person around more times for more put-downs.

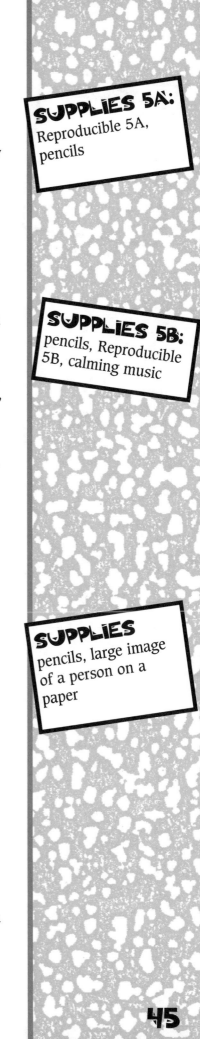

SUPPLIES 5A:
Reproducible 5A, pencils

SUPPLIES 5B:
pencils, Reproducible 5B, calming music

SUPPLIES
pencils, large image of a person on a paper

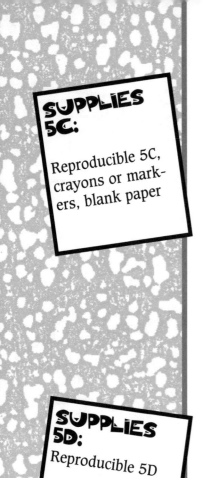

SUPPLIES
5C:

Reproducible 5C, crayons or markers, blank paper

SUPPLIES
5D:

Reproducible 5D

After everyone has torn off a piece, lay what is left in the middle of the circle and ask the students to take their pieces and try to put the paper person back together.

After they have worked with this for awhile, **say: It's hard to put the pieces back just where they were. The paper person will never be the same, no matter how hard we try. The same is true when we speak negatively about people. Hurting remarks will always stay with us and make a difference. The phrase we are studying today reminds us that God will help when we are tempted to use a put-down.**

Hand out Reproducible 5C and red crayons or markers. As the students color in the red circle and slash, talk about positive statements that can be said to help build people up instead of putting them down. Encourage them to take the reproducible home and put it in their rooms to remind them.

You may want to make additional "put down put-down" signs and place them around the church. If their schools will allow it, they may take some signs to put up at school.

Learn Song

Hand out Reproducible 5D and learn the song, "He's Got the Whole World in His Hands." **Say: Even though we sometimes do bad things or others do bad things to us, we can still know that God is in charge of the world and we can ask forgiveness and be forgiven.** After learning the song, sing it as a prayer.

Prayer and Praise

Call the class to the Celebration Table for Praise and Prayer by singing "Come! Come! Everybody Worship!" Light the candle and call their attention to the appropriate seasonal color, reminding them of its meaning. Call their attention to the circle and slash sign on the table. **Ask: Why do you suppose we placed this on the table?**

Ask the student you assigned earlier to close with the following prayer, followed by the Lord's Prayer:

Our God, there are many times when we are tempted to do something that we shouldn't. We want to remember that you can help us make the right choices about what we say and do. Amen.

Pray the Lord's Prayer together.

REPRODUCIBLE 5A: My Lord's Prayer

Instructions:

Everyone will read the phrase of the Lord's Prayer together. Then students will rewrite the phrase in their own words. The students will take the prayer home and read it daily.

Our Father, who art in heaven, hallowed be thy name.

_____

Thy kingdom come, thy will be done, on earth as it is in heaven.

_____

Give us this day our daily bread.

_____

And forgive us our trespasses,
as we forgive those who trespass against us.

_____

_____

And lead us not into temptation, but deliver us from evil.

_____

_____

For Thine is the kingdom, and the power, and the glory, forever!.

_____

Amen.

instructions:

Create a breath prayer to help you remember to ask for God's help.
A breath prayer is a prayer that you can say in one breath.

PRAYER

quiet yourself and remember that God loves you and wants you to do the right things. imagine that God is calling you by name, saying to you
" _____ ,
(use your name above)
i will help you make the right choices if you just ask."

1. Think of a special name for God that you like to use. It may be: God, Jesus, Christ, Lord, Spirit, Creator, Father, Mother, or some other name.

2. Choose a few words to form a brief sentence asking God to help you when you are tempted. It may be something like, "Help me choose what is right."

3. Combine the name for God with your brief sentence. Try placing the name for God at the beginning and end of the sentence and see which fits best.

4. Write your breath prayer on the lines below.

5. Read the prayer several times and change the wording in any way you like so that the sentence flows smoothly, as in a breath.

6. Say or think the words of the prayer as you breathe in and breathe out.

_____

_____

_____

_____

Use this prayer many times during the day, not just when you have a tough choice to make. If you use it often, then when you do have a tough choice to make you already know that God will help you.

instructions:

Use red crayons or markers. As the students color in the red circle and slash, talk about positive statements that can be said to help build people up instead of putting them down. Encourage them to take the reproducible home and put it in their rooms to remind them.

THE THING THAT REALLY MAKES ME FROWN
IS WHEN YOU PUT ME DOWN.
PLEASE GO THE EXTRA MILE
AND MAKE ME HAVE A SMILE!

49

REPRODUCIBLE 5D: Learn the Song

"He's Got the Whole World in His Hands"

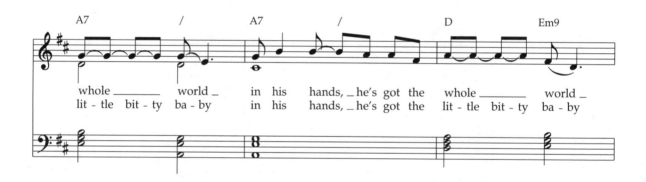

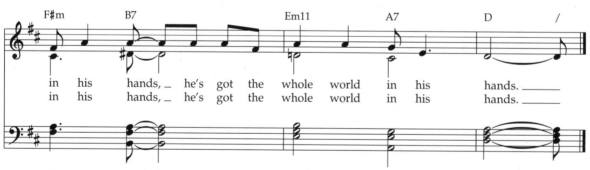

Other possible stanzas:

3. He's got the sun and the moon in his hands.
4. He's got everybody here in his hands.

WORDS: African American spiritual
MUSIC: African American spiritual; arr. by Nylea L. Butler-Moore

Arr. © 1993 Abingdon Press, admin. by The Copyright Co., Nashville, TN 37212

SESSION 6

What would God's world be like if we all lived the Lord's Prayer?

For thine is the kingdom, and the power, and the glory, forever. Amen

NOTE:
Before you begin, read the introduction, particularly the information on page 6 titled "Teaching These Lessons."

BACKGROUND:

In the first session, the students learned that this closing phrase we use with the Lord's Prayer actually comes from 1 Chronicles 29:10-13. It is a prayer that David prayed before the people not long before he died. To speak of God as the king was not a common practice among kings of that day. The rest of David's prayer speaks of all that we have as gifts from God. Read the whole prayer in 1 Chronicles 29:10-20. When we recognize that the whole world belongs to God, it makes a difference in the way that we treat the world and all that is in it.

Our world population increases, and we Americans continue to be careless in the way that we use natural resources. From the early colonists, we have acted as if resources were limitless. When things became too populated or resources were used up, we simply moved on to unpopulated land. Many of the Native American tribes had adjusted to living with a replenishing environment, but we developed a lifestyle of "using and moving." We can no longer afford to be thoughtless consumers. We must adopt a lifestyle that includes concern for the environment.

In like manner, we became an isolated country, centering on filling our own needs, even if it meant draining other countries. It was easy to feel isolated, sending some money and missionaries to other countries to make us feel benevolent. But this attitude too must change as we come to grips with our shrinking world. We are no longer an isolated nation. We are in this Kingdom of God's together with peoples from all nations. If we are to see God as our king, which this phrase in the Lord's Prayer implies, then we must claim citizenship in God's inclusive kingdom.

As you reread this phrase from the prayer, reflect on these questions:

What natural resources do you squander without thinking about it?

How can you change your lifestyle to save these resources?

Do you personally know anyone of another culture or race?

What experience have you had with people in other countries?

Whom can you speak with who has worked with people in other countries? What insight can you glean from them?

How can you help to bring about God's kingdom?

SUPPLIES:

small table,
white tablecloth,
colored fabric,
candle,
Bible,
picture of people
 from many
 nationalities,
long strip of paper

THE SESSION:
Gathering

Greet the students and, if they do not know each other, give each of them a name tag. Tell them that they are going to learn about what God's world would be like if we all lived the Lord's Prayer.

Invite an early student to help you prepare a Celebration Table. (See page 11 for instructions on preparing the table.) For this session place a picture of people from many nationalities by the candle on the table.

Ask a student to prepare to read the closing prayer in your Praise and Prayer Time.

Add to the large wall mounting of the Lord's Prayer by using large strips of paper. Today have early comers help you write the last phrase (For thine is the kingdom, and the power, and the glory, forever. Amen.) on a strip and mount it on the wall.

God's Kingdom

SUPPLIES:

Reproducible 6A,
pencils,
paper, markers,
crayons

Have the children draw a picture of what they think God's kingdom looks like. Ask them to draw places in the kingdom where they would find peace, food, water, health, shelter, clothing, love, friendship, family, worship, and learning. Discuss their kingdom pictures with them.

Hand out God's Kingdom Word Search (Reproducible 6A) and pencils. Be sure they understand the directions.

EXPERIENCE PRAYER:
Compare Prayers

SUPPLIES 6B:

Reproducible 6B

Hand out Reproducible 6B and read "The Lord's Prayer for All People" together. **Ask: How is this different from the traditional Lord's Prayer? How do the words in this prayer help you to understand the words in the traditional prayer better?**

Read the "The Lord's Prayer for All People" again as a prayer.

Form a Prayer

Sit in a circle and give each student a piece of paper and pencil. **Explain: We are going to write prayers, and each of you will write a part of a prayer as we pass the papers along the circle. I will tell you what part to write. After you write your part of the prayer, you will fold the paper over to cover that part, and the next person will write his or her part of the prayer below the fold and then fold it again. We will continue until the prayer is finished.**

Use the following parts of a prayer to guide them:

Some form of approaching God, such as "Dear God" or "Our Lord."

A sentence or phrase of adoration and worship of God.

A sentence or word about the majesty of God.

A statement of praise for what God gives us.

A confession of something that we do wrong and request for forgiveness.

A request for guidance in our day.

Another sentence or phrase of worship of God.

Amen, or some other form of closing.

After the prayers are written, tell each student to take the prayer that they just finished home and use it during the next week or as long as they like.

CENTER ON THE PHRASE:
Wall of Hope

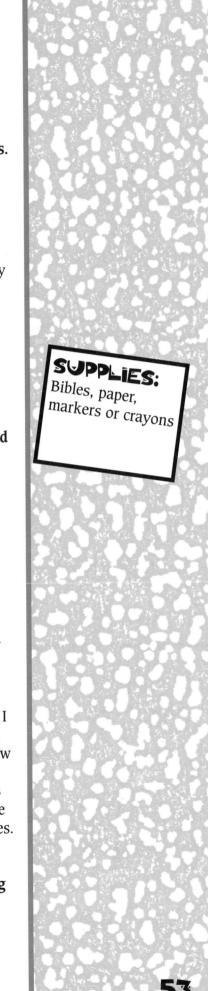
Read the final phrase of the Lord's Prayer. Then ask the students to turn to Psalm 33:5 and read it. **Say: The close of the Lord's Prayer is filled with hope. The same is true with Psalm 33:5. Look at the rest of Psalm 33 and select some part of it to illustrate. Draw a picture or write a poem that tells of hope, using some idea from Psalm 33. We will mount them around the Lord's Prayer on the wall and call it our Wall of Hope.**

Hand out Bibles, paper and markers or crayons. Review the pictures and poems as you mount them on the wall.

CENTER ON LIFE:
Hope Journey Game

For this game, everyone will sit in a circle and take a turn mentioning something in life that gives them hope. It might be an item in nature, a person's smile, or some other positive action or thing in their life. The game will be played in this manner:
The first person will say, "I was journeying toward hope, and along the way I saw _____ ." The person will mention the thing in life that gives them hope. Then the next person in the circle will repeat the same thing and add one new thing that gives them hope. This will continue around the circle, with each person repeating all that the person before said and adding one item. This is not a test for memory, so allow the students to help each other remember the items of hope. It is a way for them to continue to recognize hope in their lives. After the game is complete **say: All of these signs of hope help us realize what God's world would be like if we all lived the Lord's Prayer. Jesus gave us a great prayer, and we can live by it as well as simply repeating it together.**

Praise for Hope

Ask: When in your life can you praise God for the hope that God brings? Encourage them to think of every part of life, not just when they come to church. Help them realize that we can praise God for hope in our minds and hearts as well as with our voices.

Hand out Reproducible 6C and pencils and ask the students to design a pattern. Ask them to name each point on the pattern as a point (or time) of hope in their lives. They may write those points (or times) beside the points. Hand out crayons and say: As I play some quiet music, you will think about each of these points of hope and color in the design in some manner. Choose colors that make you think of hope and of praising God for the hope in the world.

Learn Song

Hand out Reproducible 6D and learn the song, "We, Your People, Praise You."

Say: The first and the last parts of the Lord's Prayer teach us to praise God. This song is a way of praising God.

After learning the song, be prepared to sing it as a prayer during Prayer and Praise time.

Prayer and Praise

Call the class to the Celebration Table for Praise and Prayer by singing "Come! Come! Everybody Worship!" Light the candle and call their attention to the appropriate seasonal color, reminding them of its meaning. Call their attention to the picture of people from many nationalities on the table. Ask: Why do you suppose we placed this on the table?

Allow time for discussion and help them realize that all people everywhere are a part of God's kingdom. They may not realize it, but God's kingdom is all inclusive.

Sing "We, Your People, Praise You" as a prayer.

Ask: Why do we close our eyes to pray? After suggestions are made, Say: It's not a requirement to close our eyes to pray. God hears our prayers whether our eyes are open or closed. When you ask God for help in a tough traffic situation, you certainly shouldn't close your eyes! During the closing prayer today, we will keep our eyes open and look at each other. Then when we pray the Lord's Prayer, we will look at our Wall of Hope and remember that as long as we have our thoughts on God there is hope in the world. Let's be in the manner of prayer now.

Ask the student you assigned earlier to close with the boxed prayer. Pray the Lord's Prayer together.

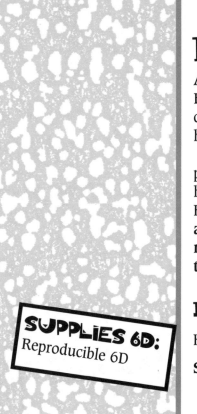

SUPPLIES 6D:
Reproducible 6D

PRAYER:
God of us all, we thank you for each person here and for our time we've had together studying this special prayer. Help us remember what we have studied each time we pray the prayer. Amen.

instructions:

Find the following words in God's Kingdom Word Search: **peace, food, water, health, shelter, clothing, love, friendship, family, worship, and learning.** These are all examples of what you would hope to find in God's kingdom.

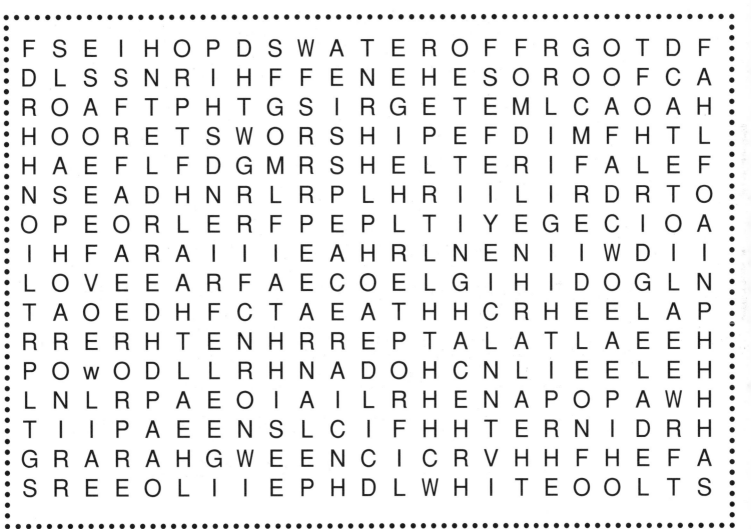

```
F S E I H O P D S W A T E R O F F R G O T D F
D L S S N R I H F F E N E H E S O R O O F C A
R O A F T P H T G S I R G E T E M L C A O A H
H O O R E T S W O R S H I P E F D I M F H T L
H A E F L F D G M R S H E L T E R I F A L E F
N S E A D H N R L R P L H R I I L I R D R T O
O P E O R L E R F P E P L T I Y E G E C I O A
I H F A R A I I I E A H R L N E N I I W D I I
L O V E E A R F A E C O E L G I H I D O G L N
T A O E D H F C T A E A T H H C R H E E L A P
R R E R H T E N H R R E P T A L A T L A E E H
P O w O D L L R H N A D O H C N L I E E L E H
L N L R P A E O I A I L R H E N A P O P A W H
T I I P A E E N S L C I F H H T E R N I D R H
G R A R A H G W E E N C I C R V H H F H E F A
S R E E O L I I E P H D L W H I T E O O L T S
```

The Lord's Prayer for All People

Our God, our creator, who is everywhere,
Holy be your names.
May your new time come.
May your will be done
In this and in every time and place.
Meet our needs each day, and
Forgive our failure to love,
As we forgive this same failure in others.
Save us in hard times, and
Lead us into the ways of love.
For yours is the wholeness, and the power,
And the loving forever. Amen.

REPRODUCIBLE 6C: Work a Design of Hope

instructions:

Draw a large design with several points in it. A star with several points might be an example. At each point write down a time when you felt hope in your life. As the teacher plays quiet music, think about each of these points of hope and color in the design in some manner. Choose colors that make you think of hope and of praising God for the hope in the world.

"We, Your People, Praise You"

WORDS: Lois Harton Young
MUSIC: ST. ANTHONY'S CHORALE, Franz Joseph Haydn
Words © 1981 by Graded Press, Music arrangement © 1967 by Graded Press.

NOTES

NOTES

NOTES

NOTES

NOTES

NOTES